Editing for Communications Professionals

Cathy Tingle

First published in the UK in 2023 by
Chartered Institute of Editing and Proofreading
8 Devonshire Square
London
EC2M 4YJ

ciep.uk

Copyright © 2023 Chartered Institute of Editing and Proofreading

ISBN 978 1 915141 12 5 (print)
ISBN 978 1 915141 13 2 (PDF ebook)

All rights reserved. No part of this publication may be reproduced or used in any manner without written permission from the publisher, except for quoting brief passages in a review.

The moral rights of the author have been asserted.

The information in this work is accurate and current at the time of publication to the best of the author's and publisher's knowledge, but it has been written as a short summary or introduction only. Readers are advised to take further steps to ensure the correctness, sufficiency or completeness of this information for their own purposes.

Development editing, copyediting and proofreading by CIEP members
Myriam Birch, Anne Gillion and Vanessa Plaister, and the CIEP's information team.

Typeset in-house
Original design by Ave Design (avedesignstudio.com)
Creative commons images from Pexels

Contents

1|	Introduction	1
	Who this guide is for	1
	Your range of tasks	2
	Why focus on editing?	3
	About this guide	4
2|	Editing: Aims and process	5
	Aims of editing	5
	A process for approaching text	7
3|	Stakeholders	9
	Your organisation	9
	Your colleagues	9
	Your designer	9
	Your audience	10
4|	Structure	12
5|	Style	14
	How to decide on your style	16
	Exceptions to overall style	18
	Tips for producing house style guidelines	18
6|	Soundness	23
	Accuracy of facts	23
	Inclusivity and accessibility	25
	Legality	26

7 |	Sense	27
	Clear writing	27
	Tone of voice	29
	Making your colleagues' writing consistent	29
	Common issues in corporate text	31
8 |	Putting it all together	42
	Working in different format types	42
9 |	Working like a professional editor	47
	Setting priorities	49
10 |	Glossary	51
11 |	Resources	54
	Branding, identity and style	54
	Clear writing	55
	Corporate writing	55
	Inclusivity and accessibility	56
	Language and grammar	57
	Legal issues	57
	Marketing communications	58
	Punctuation	58
	Working like an editor	58
	Acknowledgements	60

1 | Introduction

Who this guide is for

If you work with text within a business or another type of organisation, this guide is for you.

Your team or role description might include one or more of the following terms: campaign, communications (external or internal), content, corporate, creative, information, marketing, publications, relations (external or internal), social media, web.

You might work for a company, a charity, a council, an arts organisation like a gallery or museum, or another type of organisation entirely. You might work for a large multinational or a two-person start-up. You might work within a large communications team or be the only person of your kind within your organisation. Or communications might only be part of your job.

You might have qualifications in marketing or communications, a degree in English or another language, or no relevant qualifications at all. You may have taken courses in editing or proofreading, or you may not.

What's important is that you help to produce text that will be published in some form, from printed handbooks or long reports in Word or PDF to blog posts, PowerPoint presentations, web pages and tweets. The text you work with will represent the organisation you work for, so it will need to reflect its public identity.

Whatever your situation, if you're producing text on behalf of an organisation, you are a communications professional, and this guide is for you.

Your range of tasks

The range of what you might need to do as a communications professional is vast, and could include tasks that we won't cover in this guide, such as sourcing graphics, laying out text, commissioning editing or proofreading services, working with printers, and distributing publications once they're finished.

In this guide we will touch on the following tasks, which are listed in the order in which they usually happen:

1. creating or updating house style and other identity guidelines
2. working with colleagues or external parties to create content
3. editing content to get it ready for design and layout
4. briefing designers
5. updating previous versions of publications.

Our focus, however, will be on the process right in the centre of this list: editing content to get it ready for design and layout.

Why focus on editing?

So many communicators find ways to do their job brilliantly without any training in editing or knowledge of how professional editors work. Even so, discovering how editors approach text can be a lightbulb moment. You're likely to get answers to questions you've always had about your work, or an understanding of where to go to find those answers.

There is a world of good, established practice out there. It's something editors do all day, every day. Learning more about it is likely to make your communications better.

What does 'editing' mean?

From commissioning content or looking at the broad structure of a text to teasing out the finer points of meaning, there are many different types of editing. However, when we talk about editing in this guide we're referring to what editorial professionals call 'copyediting'.

In traditional publishing, of books or journal articles for example, copyediting is the production stage after writing, just before text is laid out in design.

Copyeditors usually work as part of a team, with publishing staff who brief them, the author who's written the text, and the designer or typesetter they'll pass the copyedited text on to. They also brief people later in the process, such as proofreaders and indexers.

Your role is likely to have similarities to a copyeditor's role. As a communications professional it's common to receive content in some form (even if only as rough notes or bullet points), to work on that content and then to pass it on to one or more team members or suppliers with all the information they'll need to publish the text.

About this guide

In this guide we'll cover five editing aims that will improve your content, then we'll look at how to approach your work using a five-stage process based on professional editing practice. We'll feature tips you can apply to make a positive difference to your communications work. At the end of the guide there is a glossary of terms and a list of resources we recommend you explore.

2 | Editing: Aims and process

Aims of editing
The main aims of editing will already matter to you in your role. That's because their ultimate purpose is better communication.

Your aims: 5Cs
Under the overarching goal of communication, editors have specific aims. These 5Cs are likely to be helpful in the sort of work you do:

- clarity
- consistency
- correctness
- completeness
- convention.

Let's look at them in more detail.

Clarity. For you, clarity is about ensuring the audience receives the message without confusion or snags ('noise'). Making communications clear involves:

- getting structure and signposting right, so the reader has a clear path through the document
- making sure text is straightforward and efficient: it says what it needs to say without using unnecessary or confusing words
- making grammar, punctuation and language precise enough that meaning is obvious.

Consistency. From branding to the details of house style, consistency is vital in corporate communications. Wally Olins, in *On Brand* (p175), writes:

> Wherever you touch a coherent brand, as a customer, a supplier, a shareholder, an employee, it feels the same.

For you, sustaining and promoting this type of identity-based consistency involves:

- making sure that the content, tone and presentation of the text fit with the organisation's brand identity
- ensuring that all text conforms to the organisation's house style if there is one (see **chapter 5**) in areas such as spelling, capitalisation and punctuation
- integrating your communications so that the look, message and style of each campaign or piece of communication is completely consistent across all formats.

Correctness. This is about trust. Your audience's trust in your organisation depends on your supplying them with information that is correct and a message that's lawful, ethical and inclusive. Ensuring correctness involves:

- checking facts are correct
- checking with colleagues that claims for a product, service or idea are true
- making sure that there are no legal problems (such as libel) in your text and that your content and language are appropriate to a diverse audience.

Completeness. This is about keeping your promises, from providing necessary information to fulfilling the brand or organisational promise every time your audience is in contact with you. Ensuring completeness involves:

- checking references and web links to external and internal sources to make sure they work and provide what you say they will provide

- answering all the questions you think your audience will have or directing your audience to where they can find these answers
- ensuring such consistency throughout all your content that your audience will get exactly what they expect every time they encounter your brand.

Convention. This 'C' changes from organisation to organisation. You will know the conventions in your organisation's field, and what certain specialist stakeholders will expect as a result. The important thing is to ensure you use specialist text only when necessary, and don't use jargon unless you know your audience expects it.

Many formats have their own conventions too. You need to include certain essential information on an information label, or structure a web page or an annual report according to agreed or official conventions. Editors work creatively within these boundaries, conforming to the rules but still ensuring clarity, consistency, correctness and completeness.

A process for approaching text

Because all projects are different, there isn't one definitive process for editing. However, most editors use three methods to keep them on track:

- They request and work with a **brief**, which should describe the purpose of a document, general style points and any special requests from the publishing team or author.
- They use **checklists**, which remind them of which editing tasks to perform, often in what order.
- They read the document several times for different purposes. Editors and proofreaders call these **passes**.

The rest of this guide will outline a process that takes in the brief and the idea of passes, and is itself a checklist. You should be able to apply it in different organisations, across different formats.

Just as your aims are based around 5Cs, the process steps are based around 5Ss. Each aim could be applied to more than one step. Clarity is particularly important in the 'structure' and 'sense' steps, for example, and consistency is a factor in them all. As you work through the steps, keep all the aims in mind to see where you can apply them.

Your process: 5Ss

The steps below define what you should think about when approaching your work, in the order that's likely to be most useful to you. For example, during the 'structure' step you'll order your text most helpfully for the audience you defined under the 'stakeholder' step; and the more detailed reading needed in the 'soundness' and 'sense' stages should come after you've decided on structure and style.

The 5Ss are:

- **Stakeholders:** Being clear about who you're working for and making sure you're meeting their needs.
- **Structure:** Ensuring your format, layout and signposting are as clear as they can be.
- **Style:** Understanding and using your brand identity, and translating it into decisions about tone of voice and the details of house style.
- **Soundness:** Checking that facts are correct, that your content and language include and respect everyone and that there are no legal problems.
- **Sense:** Making sure your audience will find your text easy to follow, that language, grammar and punctuation are clear and accurate, and that there are no typos or other errors.

Chapters 3–7 cover each process step in detail.

3 | Stakeholders

Your stakeholders anchor your work as a corporate communicator. No matter the size of the organisation you work for, you will have to meet the needs of certain people or parties. Their needs form your brief.

Let's look at who your stakeholders might be, and what they might need from you.

Your organisation

Your organisation needs you to:

- uphold and promote its brand identity, communicating the organisation's message, values and vision
- protect its reputation, helping it to avoid embarrassing or costly mistakes and language that might exclude some of its audience.

Your colleagues

Your colleagues are likely to be the people who supply you with the text you'll be getting ready to publish. Your colleagues need you to:

- make their text engaging and attractive to the audience (which might include other colleagues)
- clarify any part of their text that the audience will find unclear or misleading, asking questions when necessary.

Your designer

This is the person or team who will design and lay out your work ready for publication. Your designer needs you to:

- source some or all of the material that's not text, such as photos, figures and tables, and indicate where it's supposed to go, using

comment bubbles in Word or written instructions between chevrons: <Figure 1.1 here>
- clearly identify features such as headings, boxes and displayed quotes, using Word styles or comment bubbles. Or you could use a code (similar to an HTML code) immediately before a feature, such as <A> before a main heading, <B> before a subheading, <box> before a box and <ext> or <disp> before a displayed quote. Using codes in communications projects isn't common, but it might be the most useful method for your designer. The most important thing is that you agree with them the most helpful way you can indicate features.

Your audience

Without your audience there would be no one to read your words and act on them. In time, you'd have no organisation. Your audience really is the most important stakeholder you have. This is something you need to remember, and encourage all your other stakeholders to remember.

You're all working for the audience, which means:

- you need to gain a full understanding of the person or people who will encounter your content, and craft your communications accordingly
- obscure, complicated, jargon-filled text is at best a waste, at worst damaging
- text that points inwards, showcasing the way you as an organisation work, is of limited interest to an external audience – all readers need to see what's in it for them
- calls to action need to be easy to follow, otherwise you will lose your audience, even if they're interested and enthusiastic.

In fact, your audience is unlikely to be just one type of person. For your high-level corporate text (eg the text on the home page of your website), your readers will range from involved specialists to members of the public seeking information, so you have to pitch the language and message to meet those different needs. You'll probably need to produce different types of content for different audience groups too.

You may also have to consider other stakeholders. These might include:

- **Partner organisations or sponsors:** These are likely to be contributing to your funds, directly or indirectly, and will be keen to see their interests represented in your work and their reputation upheld. They might contribute text, images, logos or other elements to your communications, in which case they act more like colleagues.
- **The subject:** This might be the theme of a blog, the focus of a campaign or the sitter in a portrait for which you have to provide explanatory text. The subject might be a person, product or service. You need to ensure you're portraying them fairly and accurately and that they are happy to be included, if it's possible to find out.

Tip
If your text is likely to be seen by more than one audience, cater for the least specialist type. If there's complicated text, such as in an annual report, make sure there are also headline facts, summaries and illustrations to aid comprehension.

4 | Structure

Using a clear, intuitive structure is one of the most obvious ways you can draw your audience through your text and help them understand your meaning.

Some elements of structure may be beyond your control if you are working within set templates and to prescribed formats. However, there are still things you can do even with restrictions. See which of the following ideas you could apply:

- **Write useful headings and subheadings.** If they work well, subheadings provide a map for documents and improve SEO rankings (where your web page is listed on major search engines; see the box at the end of this chapter), so make sure they accurately describe the content of the section they head. This isn't the place for puns. Headings can work together to make a pattern, for example a series of questions. This helps the reader know what to expect, so they can engage with the text more easily.
- **Use short, strong introductory paragraphs or standfirsts** for each web page, blog or new section that sum up what's in the content. These could be formatted differently from body text: in bold or a different colour.
- **List the contents of pages**, particularly web pages or blogs. This will help the reader to see what's coming, and to pick out the content that's most interesting to them. On web pages, Word documents and PDFs, jumping links will take them straight to the section they want.
- **Break up long paragraphs into smaller chunks** so they're easier to digest. A very short first paragraph will draw the reader in.
- **Use vertical lists**, for example bulleted or numbered lists, to bring out points and to break up text. Order points (eg alphabetically) if you know readers will be looking for one particular thing. If they have to do something in a certain order (eg if you're giving them instructions), number your list.

- **Think about emphasising keywords and terms in bold** to help them stand out from the rest of the text. However, you'll need to be sparing about this and be able to explain – to yourself, and to your team, if necessary – what qualifies a word or term for emphasis.
- **Use pull quotes to bring out important points.**
- **Boxes or panels are useful** for summaries, case studies, extra explanation (eg glossary terms or a biography) and recurring elements in the text (eg further resources or a call to action).
- **You can use graphic elements to signpost subject matter.** These might be photographs, drawings, figures, tables and maps. However, ensure that they are ready for reproduction in the format you're working in (eg the right resolution for print); that you obtain any necessary permission for their use from the copyright holder and include a credit (see '**Legal issues**' in chapter 6); and that you make it clear to your design team where these elements should appear (see **chapter 3,** 'Stakeholders').
- **Make your calls to action clear and easy to respond to**, and don't forget to include links and suggestions for further resources.

Working with SEO

SEO (search engine optimisation) is a process to improve your web page's rankings on major search engines like Google and Bing:

- The most effective way you can do this is to think about how your intended audience might search for your offer: most likely with everyday language, not jargon. Use these searchable words, phrases and questions frequently on your web page, especially in prominent places such as headings, subheadings and introductory text.
- The other major thing you can do is create useful content and include links to similarly useful web content. The emphasis in SEO has evolved into identifying high-quality content that engages readers. Make your content rich and readable, and seek out other useful content to link to, and you'll create shareable web pages for your audience while building your SEO rankings.

5 | Style

Every time people produce text, they make choices about style, whether or not they are aware of it. Style covers everything for which there is a variant of spelling, hyphenation, capitalisation, italicisation, punctuation and its placement, and more.

If a style decision has been made by your organisation, you should be able to find it in your house style guide, if there is one.

Here is a list of possible style choices your organisation may have already made or may still need to make. Commonly used variants are listed:

- Overall spelling style
  » British '-ise' endings (organisation, realise, specialise), British '-ize/yse' endings (organization, analyse) or US '-ize/yze' endings (organization, analyze)

- Spelling, hyphenation and other variants of individual words and terms
  » focusing or focussing, benefiting or benefitting
  » wellbeing or well-being, policy maker or policy-maker
  » judgment or judgement, acknowledgment or acknowledgement
  » while or whilst, among or amongst

  There are many more words and terms with variants, and some will be particular to your industry or specialist area. If they don't appear in your house style guide, you will need to add them as you make editorial decisions about them. An A–Z list that you can easily amend (ideally online) is a good method for doing this. See 'Tips for producing house style guidelines' below.

- Punctuation
  » 'single' or "double" quote marks

- » 'straight' or 'curly' quote marks and apostrophes
- » no serial comma in a list (doctors, nurses and orderlies) or serial comma (doctors, nurses, and orderlies)
- » open en dash/rule – like this – in running text, or closed em dash—like this
- » to indicate range, closed en dash (23–24) or closed hyphen (23-24)

- Capitalisation
  - » capitalise compass points or not (North or north) and/or geographical areas or not (East Scotland or east Scotland)
  - » capitalise specialist terms and areas of study or not (Molecular Biology or molecular biology)
  - » full caps (THIS IS THE TITLE), title case (This Is the Title) or sentence case (This is the title) for section titles, chapter titles, A headings, B headings, C headings and so on. You can have different styles for different heading types
  - » capitalise after a colon in a sentence-case title or not ('Capitalisation: A guide' or 'Capitalisation: a guide') and in body text or not
  - » capitalise job roles or not, and under what circumstances (eg you might only capitalise an official title if it's alongside the title holder's name)

- Abbreviations, initialisms and contractions
  - » for acronyms: small caps (LASER), full caps (LASER) or a leading cap only (Laser)
  - » for initialisms: full caps (NHS) or small caps (NHS), full stops (N.H.S.) or no full stops (NHS)
  - » for abbreviations: full stops (Wed., Thurs.) or no full stops (Wed, Thurs)
  - » for contractions: full stops (Dr.) or no full stops (Dr)

- Numbers, dates and measurements
  - » zero to nine, 10 and above; zero to ten, 11 and above; zero to ninety-nine, 100 and above; or another style
  - » 17 June 2003, 17th June 2003 or June 17, 2003
  - » 16th century or sixteenth century

- » 10%, 10 per cent or 10 percent
  - » elision of numbers: maximum (124–5), partial (124–25) or none (124–125)

  For more on styling numbers, see the CIEP fact sheet 'Editing and proofreading numbers' (details in the '**Resources**' section).

- Use of italics and bold
  - » italics or not for films and TV and radio programmes, italics or not for books, journals and reports
  - » italics or not for non-English words and terms
  - » italics or bold for emphasis in text
  - » italics or bold for cross-references in text (eg to a glossary)

- You may also need to make decisions on issues like the formatting of lists (eg capital or lower-case letters at the start of bullet points, punctuation at the end of them), and, if you have references in your work, how you should style in-text citations and a notes system or reference list.

- For references it's a good idea to adopt a widely used system, such as the Harvard (author–date) or short-title (notes) system. Include the decisions about details, such as whether you're including 'p.' for page numbers and how you're capitalising book titles, in a dedicated section in your house style guide. For more, see the CIEP fact sheet 'References' (details in the '**Resources**' section).

How to decide on your style

Your organisation may not have a house style document, or it may contain significant gaps. Here are some tips about how to decide on missing elements or update your house style (for a more comprehensive review see the CIEP guide *Your House Style,* details in the '**Resources**' section):

- Your style will partly depend on your brand identity. If you're a British brand you are likely to want '-ise' endings, but an international company might choose British '-ize' endings (organize, analyse) because they are closer to US style and some other world Englishes.

- Similarly, certain style decisions are more conventional in the US than in Britain: full points in initialisms; initial capitals in titles; serial commas; 'percent', 'focussing' and 'acknowledgment' spelled in those ways; and so on. When choosing your style, it's useful to understand the extent of US conventions, and to consider whether they work with your identity or not. For more information about US and British styles, see chapter 21 in *New Hart's Rules* (details in '**Resources**').
- Work with existing style guides if that's helpful. There are many out there, from Oxford style ('-ize' endings and serial commas) to the *Guardian* style guide ('-ise' endings and minimal punctuation and capitalisation). Referring to an external style guide helps if a style decision needs to be made and it's not covered in your guidelines. Organisations that use this method often state that if their house style varies from the external style guide, the organisation's house style should always be prioritised. This allows for an organic evolution of the organisation's style guide, which may depart from the external style guide by degrees and then dispense with it altogether.
- In traditional editing, if an author already imposes a style, an editor will often decide on that style if it works well with other style decisions (eg if the author hyphenates 'policy-maker' and the style for 'decision-maker' is also hyphenated). If you discover a variant that's not covered in your style guide, check whether it contradicts the style elsewhere in your communications – if not, add it to your style guide.
- When thinking about things like using bold and italics in text, remember that the reader will need to understand why they're seeing them. Use them to make text clearer, for example italics to indicate that you mean *London*, a historical novel by Edward Rutherfurd, rather than the city, but don't use them for multiple reasons. Using italics for glossary terms if they're already used for titles and emphasis will introduce confusion. Always make style decisions with full knowledge of their implications for the rest of the text, never in isolation.
- Look at organisations that are similar to yours in terms of their sector, output, brand identity and tone of voice, and review their style on certain key points, such as spelling, capitalisation, numbers and dates. Even if you might not want to follow their lead in everything, there may be sound reasons for their style decisions, so take inspiration from them.

Exceptions to overall style

- Don't change spelling or hyphenation style in quotes, book titles or elements like organisation or company names ('World Health Organization' should always be written with a 'z'). However, in quoted text you can change double quote marks to single and closed em dashes to spaced en dashes, or vice versa, to match your house style.
- Retain capitalisation styles in company names (eg easyJet, first direct) and the names of other entities and people (eg author and activist bell hooks).
- In number ranges that cover teen numbers, always include the last two figures, even in a maximum elision style (312–13, not 312–3).

Tips for producing house style guidelines

You want people in your organisation to use your house style guidelines. For this, you'll need a strong vision and relevant examples. You'll also need to make the guidelines comprehensive and user-friendly, and adopt solid methods for incorporating new rules, words and terms.

A strong vision

This answers the question 'Why should I use these guidelines?' People who write for an organisation don't always care about the brand identity of that organisation. This is because they see it as mostly about graphics, irrelevant to the sort of writing they do. You need to create a clear line connecting your brand identity to the text your organisation produces every day.

Despite appearances, brands are based on words rather than graphics: it's the words describing the way an organisation sees itself (eg 'authoritative', 'friendly', 'traditional', 'quirky') that make up the brief that leads to the graphics. Introduce your house style guidelines with the rationale for the look and feel. This might include the brand's purpose, mission, vision, values, brand idea, brand story, identity principles and so on.

A good middle ground is to then produce tone-of-voice or writing guidelines, where you can talk about your brand's personality and how that is manifested in your text. This could cover aspects from the pace and flow of text, including the length of sentences and paragraphs, to the type of language to use and avoid (eg whether to use contractions or slang, whether to strongly favour the active voice, how much technical language to use) and how to refer to different aspects of people's identity. Tom Albrighton's *Copywriting Made Simple* contains these points (p252; details in '**Resources**') as part of a useful section on how to write tone-of-voice guidelines.

Relevant examples

Examples bring house style guidelines alive. You want your examples to be relevant and useful, but you don't want to point a finger at colleagues who don't currently conform to your house style, or to ridicule other people or organisations. Look for examples of misuse, but only for inspiration. Adapt real-life examples from your industry area, because that will be more useful. If you are using examples from published materials, remember to credit them.

Don't forget to include examples of good practice too, so your writers have clear guidance about what they should be doing.

Comprehensive and user-friendly

If your writers feel that you have all aspects of the organisation's house style covered, and that they'll quickly be able to find what they need, they'll be more likely to refer to your guidelines. It's a good idea, then, to make them as comprehensive – and easy to navigate – as possible.

Split your guidelines into sections. It's important for your readers to know what's in every part. Here is one structure you could follow:

1. Why your brand identity matters, and how your house style guidelines connect to it.
2. Tone-of-voice or writing guidelines.
3. General house style guidelines: overall spelling style, approach to punctuation and numbers, and so on.
4. A–Z list of principles, spellings, hyphenation, capitalisation and so on. Put everything you can in this list, as it will be the most easily searchable thing you have.

Once you have the structure agreed, create a detailed contents list for the beginning of the document.

Create a one-page version of your guidelines. And work on a version that can be viewed on a screen, or printed out to use with every new project. This version should cover the style choices most often made in your organisation, or tricky elements of style that writers often forget.

Solid methods for updating your guidelines

It's important to realise your guidelines will never be complete. New words and terms will come into use, or you will gain important new perspectives on existing ones. The arrival of Covid-19 (which can be written a variety of ways) and the widespread capitalisation of 'Black' when referring to a racial identity are two recent examples, but there are lots more. Here are some principles for updating your guidelines.

Choose a flexible format. A PDF or Word document with clear version numbers and a series of web pages are two examples of flexible formats that work with a living document such as house style guidelines. However, your organisation might already use a platform that's even more suitable.

Think about version control. You will also need to consider how often your guidelines will be revised: continually, weekly, monthly or yearly? Whichever you choose, the important thing is that your colleagues know the frequency of updates so they don't miss any.

> **Tip**
>
> Encourage your colleagues to access the guidelines online so they are always using the latest version.

Introduce style sheets. This is an essential step in engaging your writers, helping them to understand style and gaining new style points to add to your guidelines. Create a template that allows your writers both to record their style decisions and to be reminded of the existing house style. This should include a section at the top that lists your key style points, such as overall spelling style, points about punctuation, guidance on what to capitalise and more. Under that, leave room for an A–Z list for style decisions made as the project progresses. After the project is done, ask writers to submit their style sheet as part of the job.

Example style sheet

Museum of Modern Life: *Our Dogs, Ourselves* **exhibition booklet**

Writer: Jasmine Roberts

Style sheet

Source: Collins Dictionary, www.collinsdictionary.com

Spellings

British '-ise/yse' spellings (organise, analyse)

Punctuation

'Single' quote marks, "double" within
Curly quote marks and apostrophes
Spaced en dash in running text
No serial comma unless it aids clarity

Capitalisation

Capitalise job roles when part of a title
Capitalise compass points
Capitalise dog breeds according to A–Z list below

Abbreviations

No points for initialisms or acronyms (RSPCA); no point with contractions (Dr); point with abbreviations (Wed., Thurs.)

Hyphenation

No hyphens with 'non-' and 'pre-' unless for clarity, see A–Z list
Hyphens with 'post-'

Italicisation

Exhibitions, radio and TV programmes, films, books, journals, and foreign words and terms, see A–Z list

Bold

Sparingly for emphasis

Numbers, dates and measurements

zero to ten, 11 and over; numerals in measurements (eg 2 degrees Celsius)
28 June 2010
twentieth century
per cent in text; % in figures and tables
11km, 11mm
closed en dash for ranges

A–Z list of words and terms

among (not amongst)
benefited
case study (no hyphen)
chaise longue (not italics)
dachshund
dog-friendly
Dulux
en suite (not italics)
focusing
game show (no hyphen)
gundog
heatstroke
house-train

human–canine interaction
hypoallergenic
ID tag
Irish wolfhound
Jack Russell terrier
labrador
lapdog (one word)
lightweight
mid-twentieth century
mindset
nonprofit
North, the

offshoot
Old English sheepdog
pre-eminent
Rin Tin Tin
screen test
St Bernard
TV
un-neutered
Yorkshire terrier
while (not whilst)
working dog (two words)

6 | Soundness

There are certain 'sound checks' you will need to make on your text, and you should be able to do the bulk of them separately from your read for sense, which is the next step (see **chapter 7** 'Sense'). However, during the read for sense you may discover soundness issues you've missed, so keep alert for them throughout the rest of the process. 'Sound checks' are for:

- accuracy of facts
- inclusivity and accessibility
- legality.

Let's look at each in turn.

Accuracy of facts

How much fact-checking is necessary within your text will depend on the author and how responsible they feel for the accuracy of the information they have presented, but even the most thorough author can make mistakes. Search engines have made basic fact-checking relatively easy, but make sure you check at least two credible internet sources in each case.

Fact-checking can be time-consuming, and people new to editing often ask how much fact-checking they need to do. The important thing is to make sure the task is covered, so if the author is confident that their facts are correct, that's fine. Equally, if you don't have the time or resources to fact-check, inform the author and the rest of the team so they can pursue this task if they want.

In particular, check:

- proper nouns (spelling, hyphenation, capitalisation)
- historical events (dates, spelling, hyphenation, capitalisation)
- geographical locations (position, spelling, hyphenation, capitalisation)
- quotes (accuracy of reproduction, correct attribution, correct interpretation, need for permission)
- numbers (accuracy of sums, accuracy of claimed proportions or percentages, accuracy of comparisons). If you notice a problem in an official document such as an annual report, your finance team and auditors will need to be aware of your query and the outcome
- web links and references to external sources (validity of links, spelling, hyphenation, capitalisation and attribution of external sources).

Even if your fact-checking has been minimal, check that facts are consistent within the document and the suite of communications. Also, make sure your descriptions of what's elsewhere in the text (eg 'school admissions are covered in section 2.1') are accurate.

Inclusivity and accessibility

As someone in an editorial role, it's your job to make your content as inclusive as possible. You need to be alert to all the possible effects and implications of your content, good and bad, while ensuring that as many people as possible can access it. Getting this wrong can make a reader or even a whole segment of your audience feel unseen or unwelcome and, at worst, it could do them harm. Either way, it will damage your brand.

Think carefully about representation, as well as your words. Make sure you include as many different voices as possible in your communications. Don't speak for people with identities and experiences that are far from your own: consult someone with relevant lived experience wherever possible, and let them speak for themselves. The following are a few points to consider.

Referring to ethnicity and ethnic groups. Individuals and organisations worldwide are increasingly capitalising 'Black', while the umbrella term BAME (Black, Asian and minority ethnic) is increasingly being left behind in favour of specificity. *The Guardian* does not capitalise 'black', but states that any author doing so should be respected and their style kept. The *New Oxford Dictionary for Writers and Editors*, along with style guides worldwide, prescribes no hyphen in African American.

Gender-neutral language. Using 'he/him' to represent the general population is unacceptable. Using 's/he' and 'he or she' leaves out those who identify outside of a gender binary. The singular 'they' is a long-established alternative ('when a student arrives, they should report to reception'), or you can use language that doesn't include pronouns, such as 'people can' or 'visitors want'.

Disability and mental health. Research what people want to be called. If you're talking about Deaf people, it's good practice to capitalise 'Deaf', because this is what many people in the Deaf community have asked for, but don't assume this is true of an individual. Be especially alert to language that frames disability as suffering: a disabled person may use a wheelchair; they are not confined to it.

Avoid stigmatising terms such as 'crazy' or 'mad', or of using 'a bit OCD' to mean attentive to detail. These are not respectful to people with mental health conditions and they can perpetuate harmful misconceptions.

Change nouns to adjectives. As a general starting point, if you see adjectives used as nouns – 'the elderly', 'the disabled' and so on – you should change them back to adjectives – 'elderly people', 'disabled people'.

Make your communications accessible. You can do this in a number of ways, from using plain language and simple fonts, as well as alt text that allows screen readers to describe online images, to producing simplified content to parallel complex text.

See the '**Resources**' section for a list of inclusivity and accessibility resources, and use it as a base from which to build your own list. This is an area of knowledge that is always changing, so keeping up to date means always learning.

Legality

Copyright applies to any original works that are published in some form, from text to photography to music. It is automatic when the work is created and provides legal protection to the copyright holder. Content found online, including on Twitter, is included too. Any time you see that someone else's work is being used, check that, firstly, it's being fully and accurately credited, and, secondly, your organisation has permission to use it. If you've only copied a very small proportion of the work, it may fall under the realm of 'fair dealing' and you may not need to gain permission for it. See '**Resources**' for more on copyright and permissions.

In practical terms, question whether it's essential to include something that might become a copyright headache. Can the author make their point in another way?

Also be aware of the possibility of **libel** (where content has the potential to damage or defame a person or organisation) and **plagiarism** (where the work of other people or organisations is passed off as original).

7 | Sense

After looking at your project in terms of its stakeholders, structure, style and soundness, you turn to its sense. It might seem late in the process to be looking at something so important, but at this point you are ready to fully engage with the text to ensure it fulfils its purpose and that its meaning is as clear as possible for its intended audience. This chapter covers:

- clear writing
- tone of voice
- making your colleagues' writing consistent
- common issues in corporate text.

Clear writing

Clarity is one of the aims of copyediting and, as we saw in **chapter 2**, it's about making sure the reader receives your message properly.

Let's look at five pointers for clear writing.

Cut sentence length

This is one of the easiest ways to make your text more understandable. The *Oxford Guide to Plain English* (pxxvii) says: 'Readers easily lose the thread of long sentences. And the more complex your topic, the shorter your sentences should ideally be.'

Your sentences shouldn't stretch beyond 20 words for maximum readability. Try to get them much shorter.

Simplify your words

In *Read Me*, Roger Horberry and Gyles Lingwood (p82) paraphrase George Orwell's plain writing advice to count the syllables, saying 'the more syllables, the further away a word is likely to be from the clarity and power of everyday speech'.

Even if you aren't keen on syllable-counting, the call for 'everyday' language is sound. Steve Harrison in *How to Write Better Copy* (p108) comments, 'The right words are those that make your meaning clear. And the best are the ones we use all the time.' Harrison goes on to recommend using short Anglo-Saxon words (such as 'eat') rather than those with Latin or Greek roots (such as 'consume'). You can easily find lists of words with Anglo-Saxon roots on the internet, as well as other great resources for choosing simpler words. See the '**Resources**' section for more.

Put the important point at the beginning of the sentence

'We tend to junk up the beginning of our sentences with modifiers and qualifiers, making the reader work harder to discern what, exactly, we are saying', says Ann Handley in *Everybody Writes* (p25). See if you can rearrange sentences to put the important stuff first. Handley (p26) includes a list of phrases that should be avoided at the beginning of sentences. They include 'according to', 'in [year]', 'there is a' and 'it is [important, critical, advised, suggested and so on]'.

Limit negatives

Gaudy Night by Dorothy L Sayers uses a double negative in its subheading, 'A novel not without detection'. Corporate writing, however, should avoid this type of nuance, for the sake of its readers. 'Negative expressions are often harder for readers to process ... Multiple negatives can be particularly difficult' (*Oxford Guide to Plain English*, pxxxiii). Rephrase negatives as positives.

Avoid jargon

There are good reasons to avoid using jargon, according to Steve Harrison in *How to Write Better Copy* (pp135–6):

> Dishonest people use jargon. So, too, do the insecure. They fear that if they are easily understood people won't take them seriously. So they camouflage their meaning in the hope that it will lend authority to their ideas and mystique to their role.

When you encounter jargon, think how it will come across to the reader. A specialist audience might expect it. In most cases, though, you'll want to change the language to something plainer and more accessible.

Tone of voice

It's vital to get an organisation's tone of voice consistent, according to Tom Albrighton in *Copywriting Made Simple* (p241):

> Consistency paints a clear and stable picture in readers' minds of what a brand is like. Then, when the brand speaks, people think, 'I know this voice'. If the tone of voice isn't consistent, people can't remember it, or recognise it.

You may have tone-of-voice guidelines. If you do, keep them front of mind as you read through the text, to check that aspects of the writing are consistent with your verbal identity (see **chapter 5**, 'Style', for what tone-of-voice guidelines might cover).

If you don't have tone-of-voice guidelines, ask yourself if the text conforms to your brand values. For example, if one of your brand values is kindness, your writers shouldn't be cutting, sarcastic or negative.

Making your colleagues' writing consistent

Working on text written by your colleagues can be difficult. This is particularly true if they are senior to you and keen to say things in their own way, even if it goes against your organisation's guidelines. Here are some quick tips to get the best from your colleagues, followed by some points about what to check when the copy comes in.

Get the best from everyone

Inspire enthusiasm. Share with contributors what you want the document to achieve. Show them examples of great practice in similar documents.

Be clear about roles. You're the editor here, and as you're coordinating the copy you make decisions about what stays, what's foregrounded and what takes a back seat.

Make sure they read your latest tone-of-voice and house style guidelines (see chapter 5, 'Style'). Send them a style sheet template. They may not fill it in, but it will increase their awareness that the organisation has a style and that they are making style choices as they write.

Speak for the audience. Ask questions like 'Will the reader understand this?' or 'Could we make the language more accessible?' Remind colleagues that clear language will vastly increase the chances that the text will be read.

Get ahead. Try and get contributions back early, to give you time to assess what you have and get further information or ask questions. Build in this query time and share your schedule.

Create templates that people can fill with their copy. This should keep them to a certain article length and encourage them to supply specific elements like introductory text, subheadings, illustrations and further resources.

Run a workshop for your colleagues to introduce your brand identity and tone-of-voice and house style guidelines, and to explore how you can all produce good content for the organisation.

When the copy is in, check these aspects

Tone of voice. Watch for differences in formality/simplicity of language, use of jargon, and punctuation that affects tone, such as exclamation marks, commas and quote marks used 'for effect'.

Consistency of internal message. Make sure your authors don't contradict each other. This might happen if they're covering areas like names of things, people and places, dates and timings of events, and statistics. Also watch for repetition. Different contributors without an overview of the document might duplicate information that another contributor has given.

Completeness and timeliness of information. Are all the essential points made? Are all your audience's possible questions answered? If not, you will need to fill some gaps. Also, check that all the information is absolutely current. Particularly in a regular document like an annual report, contributors may have updated previous drafts and accidentally kept old information such as defunct facts and dates that have expired.

Consistency of style. Be alert to little differences in the writing. Using 'whilst' or 'amongst' where others use 'while' or 'among' is one example. It's US style to use 'toward' rather than 'towards', so if your style is British and your contributors are based in the US, make sure you look for these small style issues as well as obvious ones such as US spellings.

Common issues in corporate text

Once unclear language, inappropriate tone of voice and instances of inconsistency have been addressed, most issues in corporate text fall under one of ten categories:

1. Misleading your audience
2. Describing things
3. Lists
4. Numbers and dates
5. Quoting
6. Referring to yourself
7. Word confusion
8. Spaces and gaps
9. The details that make all the difference
10. Seeing problems that aren't there

1. Misleading your audience

All editors work to avoid that moment of confusion that stops a reader in their tracks and sends them back to the beginning of a sentence. Making the text appropriate to the reader is an important element of this work.

The other important aspect is making it as clear as possible. Here are some examples of things that might force a reader to retrace their steps.

Leaving out commas that should be there. It sounds obvious, but commas separate. This means that if there are two elements in a sentence that we're used to seeing as a unit, like 'report and accounts', we might misread them unless there is a comma to divide them:

> ✗ *This meeting is when the chair submits a report and accounts for her actions during the year.*

The words could have been better chosen, but inserting a comma fixes the problem without the need to make any other change:

> *This meeting is when the chair submits a report, and accounts for her actions during the year.*

Using a comma to try to join two full sentences. This is a comma splice, and it gives a breathy, messy quality to writing which can seem unprofessional. It can also lead the audience to expect some sort of list or description after the comma, which can trip them up:

> ✗ *She applied for the job, it had always been her dream to be a software engineer.*

If you can put a full stop where the comma is, there shouldn't be a comma there in the first place. Editors often use a semicolon to replace the comma, but some audiences may find semicolons fussy or unwelcoming. You're likely better off with a full stop and capital letter, or by adding a joining word after the comma:

> *She applied for the job. It had always been her dream to be a software engineer.*
>
> *She applied for the job, as it had always been her dream to be a software engineer.*

This sentence would also work with a colon, which is used to announce the next thought:

She applied for the job: it had always been her dream to be a software engineer.

You can find out more about commas and other forms of punctuation in the CIEP guide *Punctuation: A guide for editors and proofreaders* (see the '**Resources**' section).

Leaving out 'that'. Although it's one of those words that people like to delete to reduce word count, 'that' can be essential to stop your reader getting the wrong end of the stick. In the sentence 'The community group believes the claims of the developers are wrong', the reader has to get to 'are wrong' before they realise that the group doesn't believe the claims of the developers after all. Adding 'that' makes it much clearer: 'The community group believes that the claims of the developers are wrong.'

2. Describing things

When writers describe things, they often come unstuck in two areas: the words or terms that are doing the describing (modifiers), and the way descriptions are punctuated.

Leaving modifiers dangling:

✘ Located on the south side of the city and serving hot and cold food, you will love our new cafe.

The phrase before the comma is supposed to describe the cafe, but because the cafe is at the end of the sentence it reads as if the person being addressed is serving the food. When this happens, it usually helps to bring what's being described nearer to its description, but in this case you're better off reordering the sentence:

You will love our new cafe, which is located on the south side of the city and serves hot and cold food.

Missing out hyphens in compound modifiers. If you omit the hyphen from 'short story writer', it's hard to tell whether it's the story or the story writer that's short. Much clearer is 'short-story writer'. Remember, though, not to include hyphens with '-ly' adverbs: 'newly discovered variant' doesn't need a hyphen, because hyphens connect, and the '-ly' does the job of connecting the word to the one following.

Punctuating descriptions. If you're adding extra information or a description to a sentence, it will need punctuation before and after it to make it clear it's an aside. You could put it between two commas, like this, two dashes – like this – or two brackets (like this). In fact, it can help to think of this type of text as within brackets (parenthetical, as editors say) to remind you to include the opening and closing marks.

Problems arise when people include only one of the marks: 'Buckstone Books which was founded in 1878, is very traditional.' You need a comma before 'which was founded in 1878' because it's extra information.

Make sure you include a comma after the extra information too: 'Alex Robinson, the marketing manager gave a talk about segmentation.' Without the comma after 'manager' it sounds as if you're telling Alex Robinson that the marketing manager gave a talk. This happens a lot in text that contains names and titles, so always check this type of writing carefully.

3. Lists

Lists come up frequently in corporate text, whether you're listing the benefits of a product or thanking people for their help. Here are some common list issues.

Mistakes in ordering. Whenever you see a list, make sure it's in the right order and that there are no elements (eg numbers in a numbered list) missing. If there's no particular order, check whether there should be. Will the reader be looking for one thing, and therefore would it be helpful to put it in alphabetical order? Also, check if the current order or wording is confusing or misleading: 'The zoo boasts an enclosure for a panda, a children's play area and a cafe.' You'd be better off putting the panda enclosure last, otherwise it sounds as if everything else is contained within the enclosure too.

Use of 'as well as'. 'As well as' should only be used for items that are outside a core list. In 'this product is suitable for teenagers, younger children as well as babies' you need an 'and' between 'teenagers' and 'younger children' so it reads 'this product is suitable for teenagers and younger children as well as babies'.

Use of 'both'. This is increasingly common in sentences like 'our marketing and customer service teams both talk to each other'. You don't need 'both' here. 'Both … but' and 'both … as well as' are often used too; make sure it's 'both … and' in your text. Finally, don't use 'both' for more than two things.

Forgetting how a list started. With every list, there's a danger that by the time the author gets to the end they'll have forgotten how it started, as in the example below.

✘ *You could respond by:*

- *returning a printed form in the pre-paid envelope*
- *completing a form online*
- *send us an email to tell us what you think.*

Always pay special attention to the end of lists, to make sure they still agree with the text at the beginning.

4. Numbers and dates

You should have a clear style for numbers and dates (see **chapter 5,** 'Style'), understanding when you're using words or figures for numbers, how you format dates and so on. Here's what else you should be aware of.

Hyphens in number ranges. The convention in most styles is to use a closed en dash in a number range ('pages 5–6'). However, many writers use hyphens as they're easier to add ('pages 5-6'). Before you get your text to the designer, replace all these hyphens with en dashes if it agrees with your house style. You can create an en dash with a keyboard shortcut: CTRL+the minus key or Alt+0150 on a PC keyboard number pad; Alt+hyphen on a Mac.

Using a dash with 'between'. 'Between 1939–1945' means 'between 1939 to 1945', which doesn't work: with 'between', you need 'and'. 'From 1939–1945' is better because the en dash means 'to', but 'from 1939 to 1945' is still preferred by some editors. Talking about 'the 1939–1945 war' is fine.

Superscript ordinals. Superscript (1st, 2nd, 3rd) is rarely used in printed materials, but Microsoft Word automatically changes instances of 'st', 'rd' and 'th' to superscript after a number. You can avoid this by clicking on 'Stop Automatically Superscripting Ordinals' in the drop-down menu that appears next to this change whenever Word makes it.

Per cent and percentage points. These aren't the same. If you increase 40 by 10%, that's 44. If you increase 40 by 10 percentage points, that's 50.

See the CIEP fact sheet '**Editing and proofreading numbers**' for a longer list of things to consider when you're dealing with numbers.

5. Quoting

Sometimes you'll need to refer to the words or works of others. The first thing to do is to ensure you have permission, or that your use of other people's work comes under 'fair dealing' (see **chapter 6**, 'Soundness'), and that you credit everything properly. After that, check the following points.

Double and single quote marks. Check that your house style – for double quote marks or single – is used throughout. If there is a quote within a quote, use the opposite style: single quote marks within double, double quote marks within single. This then alternates: 'I thought I heard her say "time for a break", but then she said to me "I thought you said 'time for a break'".'

Curly and straight quote marks. If you're copying and pasting from another document, often you'll find that some of your quote marks are 'straight' and others are 'curly'. This is also the case with apostrophes. Paste a straight single quote mark into Word's 'Find' function to find all single quote marks and apostrophes. Pasting straight double quote marks into 'Find' will only locate the straight ones, which should be fine for your purposes.

Punctuation and quote marks. Your rules for this should appear in your style guide. In typical British style for non-fiction, quotes that continue a sentence should be punctuated outside the quote marks, 'like this'. There is one exception that many British editors make: 'If a full quoted sentence is preceded by a comma, colon or full stop, its final full stop should appear within the quote marks.'

Working with displayed text. How much quoted text should be displayed as an extract, and how it's presented, should be covered in your style guidelines. For example, your rule might be to display any quotes of 40 words or more separately from body text. Generally, quote marks aren't used with displayed text, but check your house style.

6. Referring to yourself

When you refer to yourself as an organisation you need to be clear about three main things: making sure you don't speak to your audiences about yourself in the same way as you might informally to your colleagues; consistently treating yourself as singular or plural; and knowing whether you include 'the' in your official name.

Your external and internal vocabulary. Many organisations use shorthand when referring internally to themselves and what they do, and you must watch that this doesn't leak into communications meant for your external audiences or more formal communications for internal audiences. This is the case with your organisation's name, which needs to always be consistent in its wording, spelling, punctuation and capitalisation. The same applies to the way you talk about your areas of activity. You might understand the meaning of your industry's jargon, or of certain initialisms you might use internally, but your customer isn't likely to and will feel excluded if they encounter it in your text.

Singular or plural. This can be a house style issue. Do you say 'the organisation is' or 'the organisation are'? It needs to be consistent. By the way, you can say both 'the organisation is' and 'we are' (from the point of view of the organisation) without contradiction.

Use of 'the'. Whether you use 'the' in your organisation's name should be recorded in your house style guide. Organisation names that don't take 'the' include Google, Apple, HSBC and BP.

Examples of organisations that take 'the' are the BBC, the NHS, the University of Edinburgh and the Society of Authors. If your organisation is of this type, don't use 'the' when using its name as an adjective: 'BBC programmes', 'NHS targets'. If you're indicating that something belongs to your organisation, however, include 'the': 'the BBC's programme', 'the NHS's targets'.

There are very few organisations that capitalise 'the' in their name. Examples are The Works, a stationery retail company, and The Venue, a hospitality business.

7. Word confusion

One important area of editing is making sure writers are saying what they think they're saying: that they have not confused their words. Here are some words that are commonly confused in corporate language.

Affect/effect. In almost every case, 'affect' is the verb ('the weather will not affect our plans') and 'effect' is the noun ('the sun has a warming effect on the rocks').

Comprises. Many writers use 'is comprised of', and this may be an accepted phrase before long. However, for now, it will reflect better on your organisation if you use either 'is composed of', 'contains' or 'comprises': 'The party bag comprises a plastic toy, a piece of cake and a bag of sweets.'

Criterion/criteria, phenomenon/phenomena. In each case, the '-on' ending is singular: one criterion, one phenomenon. The plural version ends with an 'a': many criteria, multiple phenomena.

Principle/principal. Principal is the chief, the head; principle is the rule. Think of the college principal as your pal to remember which is which.

See the CIEP fact sheet '**Easily confused words**' for more.

8. Spaces and gaps

Spaces and gaps are just as much a part of text as the words. Keep an eye on the following.

Spaces before punctuation. There shouldn't be spaces before full stops, exclamation marks, question marks, colons, semicolons, closing brackets or most apostrophes. A space can appear before an apostrophe indicating missing letters or numbers at the beginning of a word or date:

> *'twas the night before Christmas*
>
> *it was the summer of '69*

Just make sure you've used an apostrophe, not an opening quote mark.

Double spaces between sentences. Many people still automatically add two spaces between sentences as a throwback to when we used typewriters. It's not necessary these days, as software takes care of the spacing. You can find double spaces by typing two spaces into Word's 'Find' function.

9. The details that make all the difference

It's worth getting the details right. If they aren't correct, the reader might not be able to pinpoint the exact problem but they'll get the impression of an unprofessional publication, and your brand will suffer. Here are some of the details that speak volumes in your text.

Overusing apostrophes. Text like 'all mum's deserve a treat' can arise if a writer feels that simply adding an 's' to a word to make it plural isn't enough because the noun is a special one, or is an abbreviation. An apostrophe shouldn't be used here – 'all mums deserve a treat' is correct.

Underusing apostrophes. In almost every case, apostrophes should be used to indicate the person or thing that possesses something ('the student's glasses', 'the girls' club'). However, remember the exceptions: its ('of it'), hers ('of her'), theirs ('of them'), yours ('of you') and whose ('of who').

Misplacing apostrophes. Apostrophes are often misplaced in words like *peoples'* (this should be *people's* – belonging to people, not to peoples). *Women's*, *men's* and *children's* should have the apostrophe before the 's', as it indicates possession by women, men and children.

Subject and verb not agreeing:

> ✗ *The officers of the company reviews the remuneration offer.*

Here, the writer changed the singular subject ('the officer') to plural ('the officers') but forgot to amend the verb ('reviews' to 'review'). This is the sort of mistake that creeps in with last-minute amendments, particularly if there's a singular noun ('company') near the verb. Agreement can also be lost when there is a lot of extra information or description between the subject and the verb: 'The business owner, along with her staff of 63 and her accountant, go to the seaside once a year.' The text within commas doesn't alter the grammar of the sentence: it could be removed wholesale and the sentence would still make sense. So the verb should be 'goes', as it refers to the business owner rather than the people she goes to the beach with.

Overusing capital letters. Capital letters are a useful way to distinguish the particular from the general, for example Apple the company from apple the fruit. In business language, however, capitals are sometimes overused by writers who want to convey something's important or who are used to seeing defined terms capitalised in legal contracts. As a corporate communicator you will need to watch out for this, and make sure your house style is clear about when capitals should and shouldn't be used.

Using a spaced hyphen in running text. This is very common – because Word often changes the first hyphen to a dash but not the second, as here - so if you are using spaced dashes, check for rogue hyphens. If you have a 'Find' function, search for ' - ' (space hyphen space).

Use of ampersands (&) in normal text. Using '&' instead of 'and' seems like a good way to save space. But unless it's in a term or name that always uses an ampersand (eg T&Cs, Hammersmith & City), use 'and'.

10. Seeing problems that aren't there

There are some other 'rules' that you, or your colleagues, might expect to see in a list of common issues. They're not there because they're not real rules. However, these 'zombie rules' stick around in people's minds, so it's wise to look out for them. Here are some, all of which are absolutely permissible practices:

- Starting a sentence or paragraph with a connecting word such as 'and' or 'but': 'And now we'll look at the opposing view.'
- Ending a sentence with a preposition ('to', 'of', 'at', 'by', 'with'): 'What can we help you with?'
- Splitting infinitives such as 'to see' or 'to make' by adding an adverb: 'to clearly see', 'to immediately make'.
- Referring to 'data' as a single entity: 'data is', 'data shows'.

Trying to impose zombie rules can create awkward-sounding text: 'With what can we help you?' Be alert to writers who may be trying to follow zombie rules, and drop them an explanatory note if you need to. The CIEP has produced a fact sheet on zombie rules that might be helpful (see '**Resources**').

8 | Putting it all together

Working in different format types

You should be able to tackle any format by using the aims and processes we've explored in this guide, but in this chapter we'll look at how to apply a few of them to selected formats. The formats chosen and the tips suggested are far from comprehensive, but they should give you some ideas about applying what you've learned in this guide to your own work.

Tips based on the 5Cs and 5Ss

Each of the tips below is inspired by one of the 5Cs (clarity, consistency, correctness, completeness, convention) or one of the 5Ss (stakeholders, structure, style, soundness, sense). However, as we discussed in **chapter 2**, the aims and processes of editing often overlap, so other aims and processes are also likely to be relevant to each tip.

Customer-style magazines and newsletters (external and internal)

- **Stakeholders:** People are much less likely to read customer-style magazines than magazines of other types, so think what will make them read yours: articles that solve their problems, stories that look too interesting to pass by or tempting offers.
- **Soundness:** Content should be inclusive, so commission and choose case studies carefully to ensure a range of people are represented.
- **Structure:** Get the templates right for your various types of spread. A headline followed by a subheading then a very short first paragraph is a great basis for article- or advertorial-style content, according to Drayton Bird's *Commonsense Direct Marketing*. And don't forget that people might only read 'extras' such as boxes and captions, so they will need to be useful and make sense on their own.

- **Style:** Your magazine should be a vehicle where you can give your tone of voice a good run. See what you can do with it. Feed any good work back into your tone-of-voice guidelines as examples.
- **Correctness:** Get your magazine or newsletter proofread. It's likely to be a big document with many contributors, so mistakes and stylistic inconsistencies are bound to creep in.
- **Consistency:** You'll need to ensure that all the content in your magazine or newsletter links up nicely (integrates) with the rest of your comms – campaigns, website, news and podcasts – plus any product-based activity such as promotions. This means that you will need to build time into your schedule to line everything up in preparation.

Reports
- **Convention:** Check which conventions apply to your report. If it's an annual report, it will need to include official information and wording. Ensure this is in place and isn't compromised by whatever you do elsewhere in the report.
- **Stakeholders:** Reports are a format where you're likely to encounter jargon-riddled, complicated text. However, you should think about the audience member who is least immersed in your industry.
- **Structure:** All reports benefit from lists of contents, and a well-worded one-page executive summary for medium-to-long reports is incredibly effective. Within sections, list the main points in boxes, either in the body text or in a summary box at the end. Use pull quotes or similar graphics to show what's important. Use figures, tables, graphs and charts to illustrate each main point.

Signage and exhibitions
- **Soundness:** With items like museum labels, your audience wants the facts about an item or exhibit. These must be fully verified by the experts in your organisation.
- **Consistency:** Signage is often seen alongside other content – for example, a person might raise their head from an exhibition brochure to see your sign. It must therefore be consistent in style with the rest of your communications.

- **Clarity:** Ensure that your signage is visible and readable. In a shared public space, the reader might have to move on quickly. Make sure they can understand your words and message in one shot.

Social media

- **Structure:** Combine graphics and text for maximum effect. In *Commonsense Direct Marketing*, published in 2004, Drayton Bird talks about printed ads (p221): 'In advertisements, the attention-getter is almost always the headline/picture combination.' These days, this is true for social media, so make sure the juxtaposition of text and picture is surprising, or funny, or moving, depending on your purposes.
- **Consistency:** Your tone-of-voice guidelines should cover social media, but if they don't you will have to work hard on ensuring your social media posts both sound like your brand and are suitable for such informal platforms. Ask yourself basic questions such as 'Do we use contractions such as "you're" and "don't"?' and 'If we use emojis, how many, what type, and when?' Look at what you've done in other less formal formats and see if you can extend those principles.
- **Soundness:** Your social media audience is potentially huge, and no matter how quickly you delete a problematic post, someone could have captured it in a screenshot. Craft the words in a tweet or a Facebook post as carefully as you would those in a leaflet. Pay attention to facts, inclusive language and legal issues, get links right and make sure whatever you post is carefully checked before it goes out. Here, guidelines specific to social media are useful. In these, you can set out principles in areas such as appropriate content and how to post images, as well as tone of voice and emoji use.

Web pages

- **Structure:** Write meaningful headings and subheadings that clearly describe what's below them and strong introductory paragraphs containing plenty of keywords. See **'Working with SEO'** at the end of chapter 4.
- **Clarity:** Make sure the reader can find the information they want, with a linked list of contents for the page and a clear idea of where it sits within the website (use a side list or breadcrumbs to remind them of where the section is).
- **Convention:** Keep paragraphs short to reflect good practice online. Don't be afraid of one-sentence paragraphs, but vary the pace and alternate them with slightly longer ones.
- **Completeness:** Clearly and accurately link to extra information in other pages, and include a call to action if you want a particular response. Instead of vague wording like 'Find out more', be specific: 'Discover the benefits of yoga.'

Quick tips for other formats

Blogs and online articles, because they're often contributed by occasional or one-off writers, are danger areas for consistency of style and common language issues (see **chapter 7**). You will also have to watch that your brand values aren't being contradicted in contributed blogs. Include a disclaimer that makes it clear that the views expressed don't necessarily reflect those of your organisation; even so, it's always best if the blogs you publish reflect, rather than detract from, your brand values.

E-newsletters can only be sent once, so make sure images reproduce, links work and that your facts are fully checked. Also check for misleading shortened versions of the e-newsletter's title: something like 'Supporting drowning prevention' could be shortened to 'Supporting drowning' in a narrow email platform display, with negative effect.

Emails are like headed paper, so you will need to make sure that everyone in your organisation, even if they're not writing anything else, receives email guidelines. These might include ways to reflect your brand values and tone-of-voice principles (including the sort of content and language to avoid); whether and when to use specialist jargon, contractions and slang; and the use of exclamation marks and emojis. They might also cover email signatures: suggested wording; whether you encourage people to include their pronouns in their email signatures; any prescribed formatting, including logos and links; and any standard messaging, such as a request not to print out the email unless absolutely necessary.

Podcasts should be used to explore the benefits of your organisation's products and services and to build its brand identity. The hosts and guests should reflect your brand values, so spend time choosing and briefing them. Essential are supporting web notes, with links to the products and other resources mentioned in the podcast, and a comprehensive, well-written transcript in house style. It reduces clarity if you transcribe all the false starts and fillers that arise in speech, so avoid reproducing these unless they're essential to the meaning.

Videos should always be captioned to make them accessible to anyone who can't hear them. Make sure text in captions matches the text elsewhere in the video, in terms of spelling, hyphenation, capitalisation and so on. Make sure people and partner organisations appearing in the video are represented fairly. If the video covers a complicated subject, include divider slides that list the main points. If you have certain messages you need to headline, put these on slides too, to include at the appropriate point. Make calls to action easy to follow, leading to a dedicated web page that also provides back-up information and links to further resources.

9 | Working like a professional editor

We have covered many ways of working like an editor in this guide, but here are some practical tips from the editing community that you can apply to your work:

1. **Track your changes.** An editor working in Word won't start amending text in earnest until Track Changes are on. If you're working in a format that's not Word, say PowerPoint, use the highlighter function to draw attention to any changes you've made so you can keep an eye on what you've done and your colleagues can easily review your amendments.
2. **Keep the author informed.** In a typical job, editors send queries to their authors and give them the opportunity to review text changes. In the same way, you should make sure that your writers are kept abreast of changes to their text and that you query anything you're not sure about. However, like an editor does, send your list of queries once rather than asking questions one by one. This makes the process more efficient.
3. **Work in passes.** In this guide we've encouraged you to read through the text for different things: structure, style, soundness and a read for sense. Working in passes means you don't miss anything. If you see something in an early pass that's relevant to a later one, highlight the text or leave a note for yourself and come back to it later.
4. **Automate where you can.** Use the 'Find' function in Word rather than looking through your document for extra spaces or different spellings. Use templates for standard documents and create copy-and-paste text banks for wording you often use. Many editors use macros – short programs that find and correct inconsistencies and perform other time-saving functions – and software to expand text snippets so that standard wording can be added to text at the stroke

of a key. If you're in-house, you'll be restricted by what's possible within your IT system, but it might be worth working with your IT team to automate the functions you frequently perform. After all, it will save your organisation time (and therefore money).

5. **Use split screens, or extra screens.** A split screen helps you check for consistency and other issues elsewhere in the same document. An extra screen allows you to easily compare text between different documents and with information on the internet.

6. **Look it up.** We editors don't have massive brains: we just look up anything we're not sure about. We fact-check and we keep informed about inclusivity and legal issues. Create your own list of useful web links, and build a library of essential reference books for your own practice (see the '**Resources**' section for ideas).

7. **Harness the power of punctuation.** Although it's just the adding, subtracting or moving of a few small signs, good punctuation makes a difference, from adding clarity to completely changing the meaning of a sentence. Take time to understand it. See '**Punctuation**' in the '**Resources**' section.

8. **Make sure the text keeps its promises.** Check that alphabetical and numbered lists are in order and complete. If the text promises '34 ways to keep cool this summer', count them to make sure there are 34. If the text refers to something in a different part of the document, check that it appears as promised.

9. **Remember there is only one absolute rule.** Editors' decisions depend on a great number of, sometimes contradictory, factors. Top of the list should be the priorities of the audience, but you also need to consider consistency with the rest of the publications in your suite, your organisation's requirements and guidelines, and how much space you have. The one golden rule is that you need to be able to justify every decision you make.

10. **Expand your network.** Many editors work alone but alongside a network of experienced professionals who they learn from. Subscribe to editing associations' blogs and newsletters and follow them on social media. Look for **the CIEP**, the **Publishing Training Centre, ACES: The Society for Editing, Editors Canada** and **AFEPI Ireland**. Don't forget to learn from professional copywriters too: **ProCopywriters** is a UK-based organisation.

11. **Enjoy words.** Editors' and proofreaders' interactions on social media or professional forums are full of the appreciation of words. We love effective language. Read widely and deeply in all sorts of genres. Catch up with clever and award-winning marketing copy (*Read Me* by Roger Horberry and Gyles Lingwood is a great source, see the '**Resources**' section). All of this will sharpen your practice as a communicator.
12. **Never stop learning.** Language evolves. Clients' needs change. Formats are always being updated. Working processes become more streamlined. If you're advising your colleagues on publishing your organisation's materials, like a professional editor you'll need to keep learning. Read. Take relevant courses. Regularly set aside time to catch up on communications news in your industry.

Setting priorities

Editing is all about balancing the 5Cs and 5Ss to make finely judged practical decisions. The more editing you do, the better you'll get at this. However, there are times when you're in a hurry and you just need to know what to prioritise. So in our final section, we look at prioritising what matters, and what matters most is what your audience will notice:

- Make sure the text that people are more likely to read – such as **titles**, **headings**, **pull quotes**, **captions** and **calls to action** – are correct.
- Make sure you always **refer to your organisation as your house style specifies**.
- Check the **spelling and consistency of all proper nouns** carefully. Among your readers there may be people to whom these proper nouns are very familiar.

Enjoy words.

Never stop learning.

- Make sure the **sums** are checked in financial documents like annual reports. In scientific documents make sure **decimal points** are placed correctly and that **units** (kg, lb) are correct.
- Pay particular attention to **technical terms** in your field – make sure they're spelled correctly and hyphenated consistently. This will preserve the trust of your specialist stakeholders.
- Make sure **text matches text** in other formats that appear near or next to it. If there is text in a video, make sure it matches the caption that appears under it. Make sure your guidebook matches your signage.
- Ensure that **response links** and **payment systems** work perfectly – you usually only get one chance to collect someone's details or to make a sale.

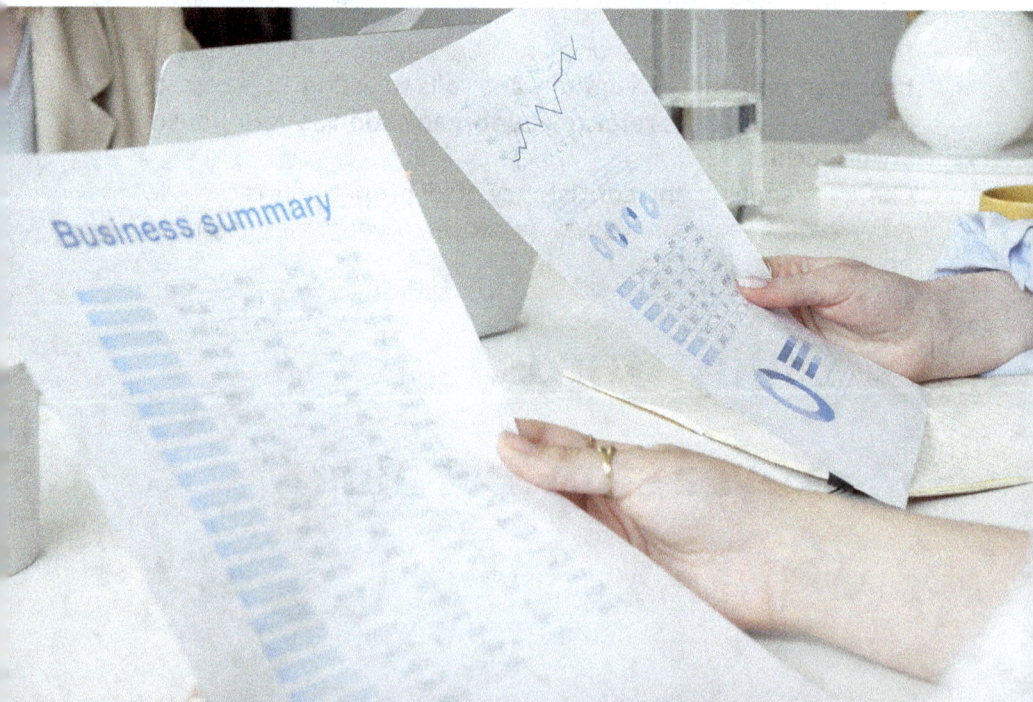

10 | Glossary

abbreviations: where the end of a word or term is cut off.

acronyms: initials that can be pronounced as a word.

active voice: this is the difference between 'we made mistakes' (active) and 'mistakes were made' (passive). It names who did the action, so it seems more honest, and it's easier to read.

adjective: a word or term that describes a **noun** or **pronoun**.

adverb: a word that describes a **verb**, an **adjective** or another adverb. Many adverbs end with '-ly'.

alt text: a short description of an image on a website that will serve if the image doesn't appear or the audience can't see it. It is also useful for SEO purposes.

body text: the main part of the **copy**, not the headlines, standfirsts, captions, lists or extra-textual material such as figures, tables and illustrations.

breadcrumbs: a website navigation method that you can use to trace where you are in subsections and sections of a website. It usually runs horizontally at the top of a page.

brief: instructions about how to complete your part of a project. Should include all the information you need, or details of where you can find it.

call to action: the part of the content that tells the audience how to respond, for example a button on a website that says 'Buy this guide'.

contractions: where the first and last letters of the word are kept but the middle is left out.

copy: text.

copyright: the exclusive right to copy or reuse an original text or work.

copyright holder: the holder of copyright, often the author or creator of a work. If you use part or all of a copyrighted work you will need to seek permission from the copyright holder and acknowledge them. In business-style communications this is likely to be with a credit.

credit: an acknowledgement of the copyright holder. A credit for an image is likely to appear in its caption or in a list at the beginning or end of the document in which it appears.

elision: leaving something out.

format: the vehicle for the text, such as a leaflet, a report, a social media posting, exhibition labels or a PowerPoint presentation.

initialism: a set of capital letters, each of which is the first letter of a word.

laying out: the designer or typesetter's task of taking the text and putting it into its final format ready for publication. This stage is followed by **proofreading**.

noun: a word or term, such as 'tree' and 'report', that gives a name to a thing, person or place.

pronoun: a word or term that's used in place of a noun, such as 'she', 'they' and 'them'.

proofreading: the stage after text is laid out, where final checks are made to catch and correct mistakes.

pull quote: a short excerpt of words from the text, set in a much larger font to highlight the point and break up the body text.

running text: text that continues without a line or paragraph break.

standfirst: one or two sentences that summarise a piece of writing, often set in larger type before the **body text**.

subject: in grammar, the person or thing that performs the action (**verb**) in a sentence.

verb: a word or term, such as 'walk', 'read' and 'eat', that describes an action.

The CIEP has a free online glossary of editing-related words and terms. See the '**Resources**' section for details.

11 | Resources

Branding, identity and style

The Economist (2018). *Style Guide: The bestselling guide to English usage*. 12th edition. Profile.

Guardian Style Guide. theguardian.com/guardian-observer-style-guide-a

Graham Hughes (2021). Editing and proofreading numbers. CIEP fact sheet. **ciep.uk/resources/factsheets/#EPN**

Michael Johnson (2016). *Branding: In five and a half steps*. Thames & Hudson.

Louise Marsters (2021). How can an editor help with brand voice? CIEP blog. **https://blog.ciep.uk/brand-voice**

New Hart's Rules (2014). Oxford University Press.

Wally Olins (2007). *On Brand*. Thames & Hudson.

Wally Olins (2008). *The Brand Handbook*. Thames & Hudson.

Christina Thomas with Abi Saffrey (2020). *Your House Style: Styling your words for maximum impact*. 3rd edition. CIEP guide. **ciep.uk/resources/guides/#YHS**

Cathy Tingle (2022). References. CIEP fact sheet. **ciep.uk/resources/factsheets/#REF**

Clear writing

Tom Albrighton (2021). *How to Write Clearly: Write with purpose, reach your reader and make your meaning crystal clear.* ABC Business Communications.

June Casagrande (2022). A word please: Flowery writing can turn off readers. LA Times. **latimes.com/socal/daily-pilot/opinion/story/2022-05-03/a-word-please-flowery-writing-can-turn-off-readers**

Martin Cutts (2020). *Oxford Guide to Plain English.* 5th edition. Oxford University Press.

Luke Finley, Laura Ripper and Sarah Carr (2020). *Editing into Plain English.* 2nd edition. CIEP guide. **ciep.uk/resources/guides/#EPL**

Plain English Campaign. Free guides. **plainenglish.co.uk/free-guides.html**

plainlanguage.gov (United States government). Use simple words and phrases. **plainlanguage.gov/guidelines/words/use-simple-words-phrases**

Corporate writing

Tom Albrighton (2018). *Copywriting Made Simple: How to write powerful and persuasive copy that sells.* ABC Business Communications.

Ann Handley (2014). *Everybody Writes: Your go-to guide to creating ridiculously good content.* Wiley.

Ann Handley. Total annarchy from Ann Handley. Newsletter archive. **https://archive.aweber.com/totalannarchy**

Steve Harrison (2016). *How to Write Better Copy.* Bluebird.

Roger Horberry and Gyles Lingwood (2014). *Read Me: 10 lessons for writing great copy.* Laurence King Publishing.

Inclusivity and accessibility

British Council. Promoting inclusion: A British Council guide to disability equality. **britishcouncil.org/sites/default/files/guide-disability-equality.pdf**

Chartered Insurance Institute (2018). Inclusive language guidelines. **cii.co.uk/media/10120292/inclusive-language-guidelines.pdf**

The CIEP. Equality, diversity and inclusion – where we stand. **ciep.uk/standards/equality-diversity-inclusion**

The Conscious Style Guide. **https://consciousstyleguide.com**

Denise Cowle (2017). Being a proofreader is not about being 'a bit OCD'. Blog. **https://denisecowleeditorial.com/proofreader-is-not-ocd**

The Diversity Style Guide. **diversitystyleguide.com**

Louise Harnby (2021). 12 ways to make your online communication more accessible. CIEP fact sheet. **ciep.uk/resources/factsheets/#OCA**

Crystal Shelley. *Conscious Language Toolkit for Editors.* **rabbitwitharedpen.com/conscious-language-toolkit-for-editors**

UK Government. Inclusive language: Words to use and avoid when writing about disability. **gov.uk/government/publications/inclusive-communication/inclusive-language-words-to-use-and-avoid-when-writing-about-disability**

UK Government. Writing about ethnicity. **ethnicity-facts-figures.service.gov.uk/style-guide/writing-about-ethnicity**

Web Accessibility Initiative. Writing for web accessibility. **w3.org/WAI/tips/writing**

Language and grammar

Stan Carey (2020). That puzzling omission. Sentence first blog. **https://stancarey.wordpress.com/2020/05/31/that-puzzling-omission**

CIEP information team (2021). Easily confused words. CIEP fact sheet. **ciep.uk/resources/factsheets/#ECW**

CIEP information team (2020). Slaying zombie language 'rules'. CIEP fact sheet. **ciep.uk/resources/factsheets/#ZR**

Philip Gooden (2004). *Who's Whose?* Bloomsbury.

New Oxford Dictionary for Writers and Editors (2014). Oxford University Press.

John Seely (2020). *The Oxford A–Z of Grammar and Punctuation*. Oxford University Press.

Legal issues

Publishers Association. Permissions guidelines. **publishers.org.uk/publications/permissions-guidelines-for-uk-publishers**

Orna Ross (2021). How to avoid libel and defamation as an author. Alliance of Independent Authors. **https://selfpublishingadvice.org/how-to-avoid-libel-and-defamation-as-an-author**

Pippa Smart (2022). Copyright. CIEP fact sheet. **ciep.uk/resources/factsheets/#COP**

Society of Authors (2016). Guidance on copyright and permissions. **societyofauthors.org/SOA/MediaLibrary/SOAWebsite/Guides/Guide-to-Copyright-and-Permissions.pdf**

UK Copyright Service. Obtaining permission to use copyright material. **https://copyrightservice.co.uk/copyright/p13_permission**

UK Government. Copyright: Detailed information. **gov.uk/topic/intellectual-property/copyright**

UK Government. Copyright notice: Digital images, photographs and the internet. **gov.uk/government/publications/copyright-notice-digital-images-photographs-and-the-internet**

Marketing communications

Drayton Bird (2004). *Commonsense Direct Marketing*. 4th edition. Kogan Page.

Chris Fill and Sarah Turnbull (2019). *Marketing Communications: Touchpoints, sharing and disruption*. 8th edition. Pearson.

Punctuation

Gerard M-F Hill (2021). *Punctuation: A guide for editors and proofreaders*. CIEP guide. **ciep.uk/resources/guides/#PEP**

Larry Trask (1997). *The Penguin Guide to Punctuation*. Penguin.

University of Bristol. Grammar and punctuation. **ole.bris.ac.uk/bbcswebdav/courses/Study_Skills/grammar-and-punctuation/index.html**

Working like an editor

Stan Carey (2021). How well read should editors be? CIEP focus paper. **ciep.uk/resources/factsheets/#HWR**

CIEP. Glossary of editorial and publishing terms. **ciep.uk/resources/editorial-glossary**

CIEP information team (2021). Getting started with macros. CIEP fact sheet. **ciep.uk/resources/factsheets/#GSM**

David Crystal (2020). Imagine an editor. CIEP focus paper. **ciep.uk/resources/factsheets/#IAE**

Amy Einsohn and Marilyn Schwartz (2019). *The Copyeditor's Handbook: A guide for book publishing and corporate communications.* 4th edition. University of California Press.

Louise Marsters (2021). A week in the life of a corporate editor. CIEP blog. **https://blog.ciep.uk/corporate-editor**

Mary McCauley (2019). Six ways an editor can improve your business content. CIEP blog. **https://blog.ciep.uk/editor-business-content**

About the author

Cathy Tingle was an in-house editor for an international educational awarding body for almost ten years, first as a publications officer and then as corporate communications manager working with a wide virtual team of communicators. During this time she took postgraduate qualifications from the Chartered Institute of Marketing and the Institute of Direct and Digital Marketing.

When she became a freelance copyeditor and proofreader, Cathy undertook industry-standard copyediting and proofreading qualifications, which she felt would have been useful earlier in her career.

Cathy is a member of the CIEP's information team and runs copyediting courses for Publishing Scotland. She has delivered bespoke online training courses and consulted on writing guidelines for organisations ranging from research bodies to art galleries.

doceditor.co.uk

Acknowledgements

First I must thank Margaret Aherne, who not only believed that I could run her copyediting courses but also generously donated her training materials for me to use. Margaret's solid copyediting principles have formed a strong foundation for my Editing for Better Communications course for Publishing Scotland, and for this guide.

Thank you so much to Publishing Scotland for giving their trainers the freedom to share our ideas and materials beyond our courses, and to training manager Joan Lyle for her understanding and support.

About the author

Thank you to everyone on the CIEP's information team: Abi Saffrey for trusting me to write this guide, Liz Dalby for expertly project-managing it, Julia Sandford-Cooke for usefully sharing her editing experiences outside traditional publishing and Harriet Power for sensitive and useful feedback. In particular, thanks to beta readers Kate Haigh and Sarah Carrette, copyeditor Myriam Birch, EDI reader Vanessa Plaister and proofreader Anne Gillion. Being on the other side of the editing process has been uplifting and enlightening. Thank you, too, to my fellow members of the CIEP. I would be lost in a lonely editing sea without you.

Finally, thanks to former colleagues Mel Pierce and Andrew Sich for their expertise and support when I was a salaried corporate communications manager, and to the wonderful delegates on my Publishing Scotland courses who have so freely shared their issues and experiences.

www.ingramcontent.com/pod-product-compliance
Lightning Source LLC
Chambersburg PA
CBHW071128130526
44590CB00057B/3382